HOW TO ENJOY R
HABITS

Your Ultimate Guide to Developing and Cultivating Enjoyable Reading Habits.

CLARENCE FISCHER

Copyright © 2024 Clarence Fischer
All rights reserved.

INTRODUCTION.

In the quiet hours of my childhood, I found solace within the pages of books. Each story became a portal to new worlds, a refuge from the mundane, and a companion in solitude. I, **Clarence Fischer,** stand before you now not just as an author, but as a fellow traveler on the timeless journey of reading.

My journey with reading began like many others'. As a child, I was captivated by tales of adventure and wonder, eagerly devouring books under the covers long after bedtime had passed. But it wasn't until later in life that I fully grasped the transformative power of this humble act.

Discovering the Essence of Reading

Reading is not merely a pastime; it is a fundamental aspect of personal growth, relaxation, and mental stimulation. Through the written word, we gain knowledge, broaden our perspectives, and empathize with characters whose lives mirror our own. It is a journey of self-discovery, where the landscapes of imagination merge seamlessly with the contours of reality.

Setting the Stage for Transformation

In the pages that follow, I invite you to embark on a journey of exploration and enrichment. This book, "How to Enjoy Reading Habits: A Guide to Cultivating Enjoyable Reading Habits," is not merely a manual but a companion on your quest to unlock the full potential of your reading habits.

What to Expect

Throughout these chapters, we will delve deep into the art and science of reading. From overcoming common barriers to selecting the right books and crafting a conducive reading environment, each page is meticulously crafted to equip you with the tools and insights needed to cultivate a lifelong love affair with reading.

Expect to discover the hidden gems nestled within the literary landscape, to conquer the distractions that threaten to derail your reading journey, and to emerge enlightened, enriched, and empowered by the transformative power of books.

As we embark on this odyssey together, let us heed the words of Carl Sagan: "Books are proof that humans can work magic." So, dear reader, let us work our own brand of magic as we turn the page and begin this wondrous adventure together.

PART ONE:

Is Reading a Skill or Habit? The Two Sides of the Literary Coin.

Welcome to the exploration of one of life's most fascinating questions: Is reading something we learn to do like tying our shoes, or is it more like brushing our teeth—a habit we do without thinking? Let's dive into this captivating topic and uncover the layers that make reading both a skill to sharpen and a habit to cultivate.

Understanding the Basics: Skill vs. Habit

Picture this: You pick up a book, your eyes scan the words, and before you know it, you're lost in a world of adventure. That's reading—a skill that lets us unlock the treasure trove of stories and knowledge hidden in books. But it's also a habit—a comforting ritual that brings joy and enrichment to our lives.

The Skill of Reading: Sharpening Your Literary Sword

Think of reading as a muscle in your brain. The more you use it, the stronger it gets. Learning to read involves mastering the alphabet, understanding how letters make sounds, and putting those sounds together to form words. It's like solving a puzzle, and with practice, you become a master puzzler!

But reading isn't just about knowing the words—it's about understanding them too. That's where comprehension comes in. As you read, your brain works overtime, making sense of the words on the page, imagining the scenes, and connecting the dots between ideas. It's like solving a mystery, and the more you read, the better you get at it.

The Habit of Reading: Nurturing Your Inner Bookworm

Now, let's talk about habits. Ever find yourself reaching for your phone without even thinking about it? That's a habit—a behavior we do automatically, almost without realizing it. Reading can be like that too. When you make reading a regular part of your day, it becomes second nature, like brushing your teeth or tying your shoes.

But building a reading habit takes time and effort. You have to carve out time in your day, find books you enjoy, and make reading a priority. It's like planting a seed and watching it grow into a beautiful flower. Before you know it, you'll find yourself reaching for books without even thinking about it, lost in the magic of storytelling.

In Conclusion: Skill, Habit, and Everything In Between

So, is reading a skill or a habit? The answer is—it's both! It's a skill that you can sharpen with practice and a habit that you can cultivate with dedication. Whether you're solving the puzzle of words or nurturing your inner bookworm, reading is a journey—one that enriches your mind, ignites your imagination, and opens doors to endless possibilities

CHAPTER 1:

The Importance of Reading Habits.

In the enchanted realm of literature, where words weave spells and stories ignite the imagination, reading habits serve as the guiding stars that illuminate the path to literary enlightenment. Join us as we unravel the mysteries of effective reading habits, explore practical tips for cultivating them, and ponder the timeless question: Is reading every day truly a noble pursuit?

The Habits of Effective Readers: Unlocking the Secrets

Effective readers aren't born—they're made through the cultivation of habits that foster a lifelong love of reading. These habits act as the scaffolding upon which proficient reading skills are built, guiding readers through the labyrinth of text with ease and confidence. Let's uncover some key habits of effective readers:

Consistency: Effective readers make reading a regular part of their daily routine. Whether it's a few pages before bed or a chapter during lunch break, they carve out dedicated time for reading each day, nurturing their literary passion.

Active Engagement: Effective readers don't passively consume words—they actively engage with the text, asking questions, making connections, and visualizing the story unfolding before their eyes. They employ strategies like annotating, summarizing, and reflecting on the material to deepen their comprehension and retention.

Curiosity: Effective readers approach each book with an insatiable curiosity, eager to explore new ideas, perspectives, and worlds. They seek out diverse genres, authors, and topics, embracing the adventure of discovery that reading offers.

Critical Thinking: Effective readers don't take everything they read at face value—they engage in critical thinking, evaluating the author's arguments, analyzing the evidence, and forming their own opinions. They question, challenge, and synthesize information, honing their analytical skills with each page turned.

Lifelong Learning: Effective readers view reading as a lifelong journey of learning and growth. They seek out opportunities to expand their knowledge, challenge their assumptions, and broaden their horizons, recognizing that the quest for wisdom is never-ending.

How to Pick Up Good Reading Habits: A Roadmap to Success

Now that we've uncovered the habits of effective readers, let's explore practical strategies for picking up good reading habits of your own:

Start Small: Begin by setting achievable reading goals and gradually increasing them as your reading habits strengthen. Whether it's reading for ten minutes a day or finishing a book each month, start with manageable targets and build from there.

Create a Reading Ritual: Establish a consistent reading routine by selecting a specific time and place for reading each day. Whether it's before bed, during your morning commute, or in a cozy corner of your home, find a quiet, comfortable space where you can immerse yourself in the joys of reading.

Choose Books Wisely: Select books that align with your interests, passions, and reading goals. Whether you prefer fiction or non-fiction, mystery or romance, choose books that captivate your imagination and inspire your curiosity.

Limit Distractions: Minimize distractions during your reading time by turning off electronic devices, finding a quiet space, and setting boundaries with family members or roommates. Create a tranquil environment that allows you to focus fully on the text at hand.

Stay Flexible: Be adaptable and open-minded in your reading habits. If you find that a particular book or genre isn't resonating with you, don't be afraid to switch gears and explore new literary territory. The key is to remain flexible and open to new experiences.

Is Reading Every Day a Good Habit?: The Ultimate Question

Ah, the age-old question—should you read every day? While there's no one-size-fits-all answer, the consensus among experts is overwhelmingly in favor of daily reading. Here's why:

Consistency Builds Mastery: Like any skill, reading improves with practice. By reading every day, you reinforce your reading habits, strengthen your skills, and deepen your appreciation for the written word.

Cultivates a Lifelong Love of Reading: Reading every day fosters a lifelong love affair with books, transforming reading from a chore into a cherished pastime. The more you read, the more you'll discover the joy, wonder, and endless possibilities that literature has to offer.

Expands Your Knowledge and Understanding: Daily reading exposes you to new ideas, perspectives, and cultures, broadening your knowledge and understanding of the world. It's a passport to adventure, enlightenment, and personal growth.

Boosts Mental Health and Well-being: Reading has been shown to reduce stress, improve cognitive function, and enhance overall well-being. It's a form of self-care—a chance to escape the stresses of daily life and immerse yourself in the beauty of language and storytelling.

cultivating good reading habits is a journey—a journey of discovery, growth, and transformation. By embracing the habits of effective readers, incorporating practical strategies into your daily routine, and making reading a consistent part of your life, you'll unlock the boundless joys and benefits that reading has to offer.

CHAPTER 2:

How to Develop Good Reading Habits.

Welcome to Chapter 8, where we unveil the secrets to cultivating good reading habits that will accompany you throughout your lifetime. Let's embark on this journey together, exploring ten actionable tips for nurturing your love of reading, sustaining enthusiasm, and embracing the joys of literary exploration.

10 Ways to Cultivate a Lifetime of Reading Habits:

1. Set Realistic Goals:

Start by setting achievable reading goals that align with your lifestyle and interests. Whether it's reading a certain number of books per month or exploring a new genre, setting clear objectives will help you stay motivated and focused on your reading journey.

2. Create a Reading Routine:

Establish a consistent reading routine by carving out dedicated time for reading each day. Whether it's before bed, during your lunch break, or on your daily commute, find a time that works for you and make reading a priority in your daily schedule.

3. Build a Comfortable Reading Space:

Designate a cozy reading nook where you can escape into the world of books without distractions. Whether it's a comfy chair by the window, a hammock in the backyard, or a blanket fort in your living room, create a space that inspires relaxation and concentration.

4. Embrace Variety:

Don't limit yourself to a single genre or author—explore a diverse range of books to keep your reading experience fresh and exciting. Try new genres, revisit old favorites, and be open to discovering hidden literary gems you might not have considered before.

5. Keep Track of Your Progress:

Keep a reading journal or use a tracking app to record the books you've read, jot down your thoughts and reflections, and set new reading goals. Tracking your progress will not only help you stay organized but also provide a sense of accomplishment as you see how far you've come.

6. Join a Book Club:

Joining a book club or reading group is a fantastic way to connect with other readers, discover new books, and engage in lively discussions. Whether it's an in-person club or an online community, sharing your love of reading with others can enhance your reading experience and introduce you to diverse perspectives.

7. Experiment with Different Formats:

Explore different reading formats, such as print books, e-books, and audiobooks, to find what works best for you. Each format offers a unique reading experience, and switching things up can help prevent boredom and keep your enthusiasm for reading alive.

8. Set Aside Time for Exploratory Reading:

Make time for exploratory reading—delve into genres or topics you're curious about but haven't explored before. Take a chance on a book outside your comfort zone, and you may be pleasantly surprised by what you discover.

9. Reconnect with Old Favorites:

Revisit beloved books from your past and rediscover the magic that first captivated you. Whether it's a childhood favorite or a book that holds special memories, reconnecting with old favorites can reignite your passion for reading and remind you why you fell in love with books in the first place.

10. Share Your Love of Reading:

Share your love of reading with others—recommend books to friends and family, participate in book discussions, and engage with fellow readers on social media. Sharing your reading experiences not only fosters connections but also spreads the joy of reading to others.

Sustaining Enthusiasm for Reading Over the Long Term:

Set Realistic Expectations: Don't pressure yourself to read a certain number of books or meet specific reading goals. Enjoy the journey of reading at your own pace and savor each book for its unique qualities.

Mix Up Your Reading Routine: Keep your reading habits fresh and exciting by alternating between genres, formats, and authors. Experiment with different styles of writing and storytelling to keep your reading experience varied and engaging.

Stay Curious: Cultivate a sense of curiosity and wonder about the world of books. Explore new genres, topics, and authors that pique your interest, and never stop seeking out new reading adventures.

Celebrate Milestones: Celebrate your reading milestones, whether it's finishing a book, reaching a reading goal, or discovering a new favorite author. Acknowledge your progress and take pride in your reading accomplishments.

Connect with Fellow Readers: Surround yourself with fellow book lovers who share your passion for reading. Engage in discussions about books, exchange recommendations, and celebrate your shared love of literature.

Exploring New Genres, Revisiting Old Favorites, and Sharing Your Love of Reading:

Explore New Genres: Step outside your comfort zone and explore new genres that you haven't tried before. Whether it's science fiction, historical fiction, or mystery, broaden your reading horizons and discover new literary worlds to explore.

Revisit Old Favorites: Revisit old favorite books and authors that hold a special place in your heart. Rereading familiar stories can evoke feelings of nostalgia and rekindle your love for reading.

Share Your Love of Reading: Share your passion for reading with others by recommending books, starting conversations about literature, and participating in reading-related activities. Spread the joy of reading and inspire others to embark on their own reading adventures.

cultivating good reading habits is a journey—a journey of discovery, growth, and transformation. By embracing these ten transformative ways to cultivate reading habits, sustaining your enthusiasm for reading over the long term, and sharing your love of reading with others, you'll unlock the boundless joys and benefits that will enrich your life and bring you endless joy and fulfillment

CHAPTER 3:

Exploring Factors Affecting Reading Habits.

In the intricate tapestry of our lives, countless factors shape our reading habits—some visible, others hidden beneath the surface. Join us on a journey of exploration as we unravel the multifaceted influences that impact how, when, and why we engage with books. From personal preferences and societal pressures to technological advancements and environmental factors, let's delve into the complex ecosystem of reading habits and discover the forces at play.

1. Personal Preferences:

Our individual tastes, interests, and inclinations play a significant role in shaping our reading habits. Whether we gravitate towards fiction or non-fiction, romance or mystery, our preferences influence the types of books we choose to read and the frequency with which we engage in reading.

2. Time Constraints:

In today's fast-paced world, time is a precious commodity, and competing demands often encroach upon our reading habits. Work responsibilities, family obligations, and social commitments can leave little time for leisurely pursuits like reading, making it challenging to prioritize and maintain consistent reading habits.

3. Digital Distractions:

The proliferation of digital devices and online entertainment has transformed the reading landscape, introducing new distractions and temptations that vie for our attention. Social media, streaming services, and mobile games compete for our time and mental bandwidth, diverting our focus away from sustained reading.

4. Environmental Factors:

Our physical environment can significantly impact our reading habits, influencing factors such as comfort, noise levels, and accessibility to reading materials. A quiet, well-lit space conducive to concentration can facilitate immersive reading experiences, while distractions and discomfort may hinder our ability to engage with books effectively.

5. Socioeconomic Status:

Socioeconomic factors, such as income level, education, and access to resources, can influence reading habits and preferences. Individuals from privileged backgrounds may have greater access to books, educational opportunities, and leisure time for reading, while those facing economic challenges may encounter barriers to accessing reading materials and developing reading habits.

6. Social Influences:

Our social networks, including family, friends, and peers, can shape our reading habits through recommendations, discussions, and cultural norms. Book clubs, reading groups, and online communities provide opportunities for social engagement and collective exploration of reading interests, influencing our reading choices and behaviors.

7. Technological Advancements:

Advancements in technology have revolutionized the way we consume and interact with written content, offering a plethora of digital platforms, e-books, and audiobooks that expand our reading options and preferences. While technology enhances accessibility and convenience, it also introduces challenges such as screen fatigue and information overload that may impact reading habits.

8. Psychological Factors:

Psychological factors, including motivation, self-discipline, and mindset, play a crucial role in shaping reading habits. A positive attitude towards reading, intrinsic motivation, and a growth mindset that values continuous learning can foster a lifelong love of reading and sustain enthusiasm for literary exploration.

In conclusion, reading habits are influenced by a complex interplay of personal, social, environmental, and technological factors that shape our engagement with books. By understanding the multifaceted influences at play, we can identify opportunities for fostering positive reading habits, overcoming challenges, and embracing a lifelong journey of literary discovery and enrichment.

CHAPTER 4:

The Bad Reading Habits

In the History of our reading lives, there exist threads of both virtue and vice—habits that uplift and habits that hinder. In this chapter, we shall shine a light on the shadows cast by bad reading habits, identifying their insidious forms and unraveling the consequences they bear on our literary journey.

Identifying Bad Reading Habits:

Procrastination: The perennial thief of time, procrastination robs us of precious reading opportunities. Whether it's putting off starting a book, delaying reading sessions, or constantly postponing finishing a book, procrastination prevents us from fully immersing ourselves in the joys of reading.

Distraction: In an age of constant connectivity, distractions lurk around every corner, ready to snatch our attention away from the pages of a book. Whether it's the siren song of social media, the allure of streaming services, or the incessant buzzing of notifications, succumbing to distractions disrupts our reading flow and impedes our comprehension.

Speed Reading: While the ability to read quickly can be advantageous in certain contexts, speed reading at the expense of comprehension is a harmful habit. Skimming through pages without pausing to reflect, digest, and savor the content diminishes our understanding and robs us of the deeper insights that literature has to offer.

Multitasking: Attempting to multitask while reading—whether it's watching TV, scrolling through social media, or engaging in other activities—divides our attention and dilutes our focus. Instead of fully immersing ourselves in the world of the book, we spread ourselves thin, compromising both the quality of our reading experience and our ability to retain information.

Overreliance on Summaries: Relying too heavily on book summaries, reviews, or online synopses to glean information about a book without actually reading it undermines our ability to engage directly with the text. While summaries can provide valuable insights, they should complement, not replace, the act of reading itself.

The Effects of Bad Reading Habits:

Reduced Comprehension: Bad reading habits impede our ability to comprehend and internalize the material we read. Whether it's skimming through pages, succumbing to distractions, or multitasking while reading, these habits compromise our understanding of the text and hinder our ability to derive meaning from it.

Diminished Enjoyment: Reading is not just about extracting information—it's about immersing ourselves in the beauty of language, the depth of storytelling, and the richness of ideas. Bad reading habits detract from our enjoyment of the reading experience, turning it into a chore rather than a pleasure.

Impaired Retention: When we rush through books or allow ourselves to be constantly distracted, we fail to fully absorb and retain the information presented to us. As a result, our memory of the text is fleeting, and the insights we gain from it are quickly forgotten.

Stunted Growth: Reading is a journey of personal and intellectual growth—a process of exploration, discovery, and self-reflection. Bad reading habits hinder our growth by limiting our exposure to new ideas, perspectives, and experiences, constraining our ability to broaden our horizons and expand our understanding of the world.

Missed Opportunities: Ultimately, bad reading habits rob us of the myriad opportunities that reading affords us—to learn, to grow, to be entertained, and to connect with others. They stand as barriers between us and the transformative power of the written word, preventing us from fully realizing our potential as readers and as individuals.

Strategies for Overcoming Bad Reading Habits:

Set Clear Goals: Establish specific, achievable reading goals that align with your interests and priorities. Break larger reading tasks into smaller, manageable steps to avoid feeling overwhelmed.

Create a Distraction-Free Environment: Minimize distractions by setting aside dedicated time and space for reading. Silence notifications, put away electronic devices, and create a calm, quiet atmosphere conducive to focused reading.

Practice Active Reading: Engage with texts actively by employing strategies such as annotating, summarizing, and reflecting on the material. Take notes, ask questions, and make connections to deepen comprehension and retention.

Manage Time Effectively: Prioritize reading in your daily schedule and allocate specific time blocks for reading activities. Use time management techniques, such as the Pomodoro Technique, to break reading sessions into focused intervals with short breaks in between.

Diversify Your Reading: Explore diverse genres, authors, and formats to keep your reading experience varied and engaging. Step outside your comfort zone and challenge yourself to read books that broaden your horizons and expand your literary palate.

Practice Mindfulness: Cultivate mindfulness during reading sessions by staying present and focused on the text. Notice any wandering thoughts or distractions and gently redirect your attention back to the material.

Seek Support: Join a book club, reading group, or online community where you can connect with fellow readers, share reading experiences, and receive encouragement and accountability.

Reward Yourself: Celebrate your progress and achievements by rewarding yourself with small treats or incentives for reaching reading milestones or overcoming challenges.

bad reading habits are like weeds in the garden of our literary lives—choking the flowers of curiosity, stifling the fruits of knowledge, and casting shadows over the landscape of our reading journey. By identifying and confronting these habits, we can cultivate a fertile soil in which our love of reading can thrive, unfettered by vice and nourished by virtue.

PART TWO:

How Can I Enjoy Reading Better? Unveiling the Secrets to a Fulfilling Reading Experience.

Welcome to Part Two, where we delve into the art of enjoying reading to its fullest. Let's embark on a journey to uncover practical tips and delightful strategies that will enrich your reading adventures and transform the way you experience books. Get ready to dive deep into the world of literature and discover the keys to unlocking a truly enjoyable reading experience.

1. Cultivate Curiosity:

Fuel your reading journey with curiosity, the spark that ignites the flames of exploration. Approach each book with an open mind and a sense of wonder, eager to uncover new ideas, worlds, and perspectives. Let curiosity be your guiding light as you navigate the vast landscape of literature, and watch as it leads you to unexpected treasures and enriching discoveries.

2. Engage All Your Senses:

Immerse yourself fully in the world of books by engaging all your senses. Visualize the scenes unfolding before you, hear the characters' voices in your mind, and feel the texture of the pages beneath your fingertips. By awakening your senses, you'll deepen your connection to the story and bring the words on the page to life in vibrant detail.

3. Create a Cozy Reading Environment:

Transform your reading space into a cozy sanctuary where you can escape the noise and distractions of the outside world. Surround yourself with soft blankets, plump pillows, and warm lighting to create a tranquil oasis where you can lose yourself in the pages of a good book. By creating a cozy reading environment, you'll enhance your comfort and concentration, making it easier to immerse yourself in the story.

4. Embrace Variety:

Diversify your reading diet by exploring a wide range of genres, authors, and styles. Whether you're drawn to pulse-pounding thrillers, heartwarming romances, or thought-provoking literary fiction, there's a book out there waiting to capture your imagination. By embracing variety in your reading choices, you'll keep your reading experience fresh and exciting, and discover new favorites along the way.

5. Make Reading a Ritual:

Carve out dedicated time for reading each day and make it a cherished part of your routine. Whether it's the quiet moments before bed, a leisurely afternoon break, or the peaceful hours of the morning, find a time that works for you and commit to it. By making reading a ritual, you'll create a sense of anticipation and enjoyment, and ensure that it becomes an integral part of your daily life.

6. Practice Mindful Reading:

Engage in mindful reading by immersing yourself fully in the present moment and savoring each word and phrase with intention and awareness. Slow down your reading pace, pause to reflect on the meaning of the text, and allow yourself to be fully absorbed in the story. By practicing mindful reading, you'll deepen your appreciation for the nuances of language and enrich your reading experience.

7. Connect with Others:

Share your love of reading with friends, family, and fellow book lovers. Join book clubs, attend author events, and participate in online discussions to connect with others who share your passion for literature. By engaging in meaningful conversations about books, you'll gain new insights, discover different perspectives, and forge connections that enhance your reading enjoyment.

8. Reflect and Revisit:

Take time to reflect on your reading experiences and revisit books that have left a lasting impression on you. Keep a reading journal to record your thoughts, feelings, and favorite passages, and revisit them whenever you need a dose of literary inspiration. By reflecting on your reading journey, you'll gain valuable insights into your own tastes and preferences, and deepen your appreciation for the power of storytelling.

In conclusion, enjoying reading is an art form—a delightful journey of exploration, discovery, and connection. By cultivating curiosity, engaging your senses, creating a cozy reading environment, embracing variety, making reading a ritual, practicing mindful reading, connecting with others, and reflecting on your experiences, you'll unlock the secrets to a truly fulfilling reading experience.

CHAPTER 5:

How Can I Improve My Reading Habit? Unveiling the Path to Reading Mastery

In this chapter, we embark on a journey to unlock the secrets of improving your reading habit. We'll explore practical strategies and invaluable insights that will empower you to become a master of the written word. Get ready to enhance your reading experience, deepen your understanding, and unlock the countless benefits of developing good reading habits.

Improving Your Reading Habit: Practical Strategies for Success

Set Realistic Goals: Begin by setting achievable reading goals that align with your interests and schedule. Whether it's reading for 20 minutes each day or finishing a book per week, setting realistic targets will help you stay motivated and track your progress.

Establish a Routine: Make reading a regular part of your daily routine by setting aside dedicated time for it. Whether it's in the morning before work, during your lunch break, or before bed, find a time that works for you and stick to it consistently.

Create a Reading Environment: Designate a comfortable and quiet space where you can immerse yourself in your reading. Remove distractions, such as electronic devices or noisy surroundings, and create a cozy atmosphere that encourages focus and relaxation.

Choose Engaging Content: Select books and articles that capture your interest and enthusiasm. Whether it's fiction, non-fiction, or poetry, choose reading material that resonates with you and sparks your curiosity.

Practice Active Reading: Engage actively with the text by asking questions, making connections, and taking notes as you read. Use techniques like highlighting, annotating, and summarizing to deepen your understanding and retention of the material.

Expand Your Vocabulary: Challenge yourself to learn new words and phrases by reading diverse genres and authors. Keep a dictionary handy to look up unfamiliar terms and incorporate them into your vocabulary.

Join a Reading Group: Consider joining a book club or reading group to connect with other readers and discuss your favorite books. Sharing insights and perspectives with fellow book lovers can enhance your enjoyment of reading and expose you to new ideas.

Set Aside Distraction-Free Time: Create a daily reading ritual where you disconnect from technology and immerse yourself in the world of books. By setting aside distraction-free time, you can fully focus on your reading and reap the benefits of uninterrupted immersion.

The Benefits of Developing Good Reading Habits

Enhanced Knowledge and Understanding: Reading exposes you to a wealth of information, ideas, and perspectives, broadening your knowledge and deepening your understanding of the world around you.

Improved Vocabulary and Language Skills: Regular reading expands your vocabulary and enhances your language proficiency, making you a more effective communicator and writer.

Stress Reduction and Relaxation: Engaging in a good book provides an opportunity to escape from the stresses of daily life and unwind in a world of imagination and creativity.

Increased Empathy and Understanding: Reading fiction allows you to step into the shoes of different characters and experience their thoughts, emotions, and struggles, fostering empathy and understanding.

Enhanced Critical Thinking Skills: Analyzing and evaluating the content of what you read encourages critical thinking and problem-solving skills, helping you become a more discerning and thoughtful reader.

Cognitive Stimulation and Brain Health: Regular reading exercises your brain, keeping it active and engaged, and may even help stave off cognitive decline and dementia as you age.

Personal Growth and Development: Reading exposes you to new ideas, perspectives, and experiences, fostering personal growth, self-reflection, and continuous learning throughout your life.

improving your reading habit is a journey of self-discovery and lifelong learning. By implementing practical strategies and embracing the benefits of good reading habits, you can enrich your mind, broaden your horizons, and unlock the endless joys of the written word

CHAPTER 6:

Understanding Your Reading Preferences.

In this chapter, we embark on a journey of self-discovery to uncover your unique reading preferences. By exploring different genres, reflecting on past reading experiences, and discovering new authors, you'll gain valuable insights into what resonates most with you as a reader.

Exploring Different Genres and Styles.

To understand your reading preferences, it's essential to explore a variety of genres and styles. From thrilling mysteries to heartwarming romances, each genre offers a unique experience that may appeal to different aspects of your personality and interests. Take the time to dip your toes into various genres and pay attention to how each makes you feel. Do you find yourself captivated by the suspense of a mystery novel, or do you prefer the escapism of fantasy? By exploring different genres, you'll gain a better understanding of what types of stories resonate with you.

Assessing Past Reading Experiences

Reflecting on past reading experiences can provide valuable insights into your preferences as a reader. Think back to books you've enjoyed in the past and consider what elements made them memorable for you. Was it the compelling characters, the intricate plot twists, or the lyrical prose? Pay attention to recurring themes, settings, or writing styles that have resonated with you in the past. By assessing your past reading experiences, you'll uncover patterns and themes that can help guide your future reading choices.

Tips for Discovering New Genres and Authors

Discovering new genres and authors aligned with your individual tastes can open up a world of literary possibilities. Here are some tips to help you expand your reading horizons:

Ask for Recommendations: Reach out to friends, family, or fellow book lovers for recommendations based on your interests and preferences. You may discover hidden gems and new favorites that you wouldn't have found on your own.

Explore Book Lists and Awards: Browse book lists, literary awards, and bestseller lists to discover popular books and authors within different genres. Pay attention to award-winning titles or books that receive critical acclaim, as they may align with your tastes.

Join Online Communities: Join online book clubs, forums, or social media groups dedicated to discussing books and sharing recommendations. Engaging with other readers can expose you to diverse perspectives and introduce you to books you might not have discovered otherwise.

Visit Your Local Library or Bookstore: Take a trip to your local library or bookstore and explore the shelves to discover new books and authors. Librarians and booksellers can also offer personalized recommendations based on your interests and reading preferences.

Experiment with Different Formats: Experiment with different formats, such as audiobooks or graphic novels, to explore new genres and styles. You may find that certain formats enhance your reading experience and open up new avenues for exploration.

By actively exploring different genres and styles, reflecting on past reading experiences, and seeking out new authors and books, you'll gain a deeper understanding of your unique reading preferences. Embrace the journey of discovery and allow yourself to be open to new experiences, and you'll unlock a world of literary treasures tailored to your individual tastes.

CHAPTER 7:

Creating Your Ideal Reading Environment.

In this chapter, we will explore the art of crafting a perfect reading sanctuary where you can escape into the world of books and indulge in the joy of reading. From selecting the right ambiance to arranging your seating for comfort, we'll provide practical advice on how to design a space that enhances your reading experience and makes it truly enjoyable.

Designing a Comfortable and Conducive Reading Environment at Home

Your reading environment plays a crucial role in shaping your reading experience. Here's how you can create a space that invites you to relax, unwind, and immerse yourself in the pages of a good book:

Selecting the Right Location: Choose a quiet and cozy corner of your home where you can retreat from distractions and interruptions. Whether it's a sunny spot by the window, a nook under the stairs, or a corner of your bedroom, find a space that feels inviting and conducive to concentration.

Creating Ambiance: Set the mood with elements of ambiance that appeal to your senses. Consider adding soft lighting, such as floor lamps or string lights, to create a warm and inviting atmosphere. You can also incorporate candles, essential oil diffusers, or your favorite scents to enhance relaxation and set the tone for your reading experience.

Optimizing Seating Arrangements: Choose comfortable seating options that provide adequate support and relaxation. Whether it's a plush armchair, a cozy bean bag chair, or a pile of floor cushions, select seating that allows you to sink in and get lost in your book without discomfort.

Incorporating Elements of Ambiance, Lighting, and Seating Arrangements for Optimal Enjoyment

Lighting: Good lighting is essential for reading comfortably and avoiding eye strain. Opt for natural light during the day by positioning your reading nook near a window. In the evening or in darker spaces, supplement with soft, diffused lighting sources like adjustable lamps or string lights to create a cozy atmosphere without harsh glare.

Ambiance: Set the mood with ambient elements that appeal to your senses and enhance relaxation. Consider adding soothing background music, nature sounds, or ambient noise apps to create a calming auditory backdrop. You can also incorporate decorative touches like plants, artwork, or cozy textiles to add visual interest and make your reading nook feel inviting and personal.

Seating Arrangements: Choose seating options that prioritize comfort and support to ensure long hours of uninterrupted reading pleasure. Look for ergonomic chairs or sofas with firm cushions and adequate lumbar support to promote good posture and prevent discomfort. Consider adding additional seating options like ottomans, poufs, or floor cushions for versatility and flexibility in your reading space.

Practical Advice for Organizing and Personalizing Your Reading Nook

Organize Your Library: Arrange your books in a way that makes them easily accessible and visually pleasing. Consider organizing them by genre, author, or theme, and use bookshelves, floating shelves, or storage bins to keep them tidy and organized.

Personalize Your Space: Infuse your reading nook with personal touches that reflect your interests, passions, and personality. Display cherished items like family photos, travel souvenirs, or sentimental objects that bring you joy and inspire you to linger in your reading space.

Minimize Distractions: Create a distraction-free environment by decluttering your space and removing unnecessary items that might divert your attention from your reading. Keep electronic devices, like phones, tablets, or laptops, out of sight or on silent mode to minimize interruptions and maintain focus.

creating your ideal reading environment is all about designing a space that caters to your comfort, relaxation, and enjoyment. By incorporating elements of ambiance, lighting, seating arrangements, and personalization, you can transform any corner of your home into a cozy sanctuary where you can escape into the magical world of books.

CHAPTER 8:

Exploring Diverse Reading Formats

In this chapter, we'll embark on a journey to explore the diverse world of reading formats, from traditional print books to digital e-books and immersive audiobooks. We'll delve into the advantages and considerations of each format, empowering you to make informed choices based on your preferences and reading circumstances. Let's dive in and discover the wonders of different reading formats together.

Overview of Various Reading Formats

Print Books: Traditional print books have been beloved companions for centuries, offering a tangible and tactile reading experience. With their crisp pages, comforting smell, and satisfying weight in hand, print books appeal to many readers who cherish the sensory pleasure of flipping through physical pages and holding a book in their hands.

E-books: E-books have revolutionized the way we read, providing convenient access to a vast library of digital titles that can be stored and carried in a single device. With e-books, readers can enjoy instant access to their favorite books anytime, anywhere, and customize their reading experience with features like adjustable font sizes, bookmarks, and built-in dictionaries.

Audiobooks: Audiobooks offer a unique reading experience by bringing stories to life through spoken narration and sound effects. Ideal for multitasking or on-the-go listening, audiobooks allow readers to immerse themselves in a story while commuting, exercising, or completing household chores, making them a convenient option for busy readers.

Advantages and Considerations for Each Format

◇ **Print Books:**

◇ **Advantages:** Tangible, sensory experience; no reliance on technology; ability to easily annotate and flip through pages.

◇ **Considerations:** Physical storage space required; less portable than digital formats; potential eye strain for prolonged reading.

◇ **E-books:**

◈ **Advantages:** Portable and space-saving; customizable reading experience; access to a vast digital library; built-in features like adjustable font sizes and search functions.

◈ **Considerations:** Dependence on electronic devices; potential for screen fatigue; compatibility issues with certain e-readers or devices.

◈ **Audiobooks:**

◈ **Advantages:** Hands-free reading experience; ideal for multitasking; accessibility for visually impaired readers; immersive storytelling through narration and sound effects.

◈ **Considerations:** Dependency on audio technology; pacing determined by narrator; potential distractions in noisy environments.

Guidance for Transitioning Between Different Formats

Assess Your Reading Context: Consider your reading environment, schedule, and preferences when choosing a reading format. Opt for print books when seeking a tactile experience or e-books for on-the-go convenience. Reserve audiobooks for times when multitasking or commuting.

Experiment and Explore: Don't be afraid to experiment with different formats to discover what works best for you in different situations. Try listening to audiobooks during your daily commute, reading e-books on your tablet before bed, and savoring print books for leisurely weekend reading sessions.

Be Open to Adaptation: Remain flexible and open-minded about transitioning between formats as your circumstances and preferences evolve. Embrace the versatility of each format and adapt your reading habits accordingly to suit your changing needs and lifestyle.

exploring diverse reading formats opens up a world of possibilities and enriches your reading experience in unique ways. By understanding the advantages and considerations of print books, e-books, and audiobooks, and embracing the flexibility to transition between formats, you can tailor your reading habits to suit your preferences and circumstances.

CHAPTER 9:

Setting and Achieving Reading Goals.

In this chapter, we will dive into the process of setting and achieving reading goals, empowering you to embark on a fulfilling journey of literary exploration. From establishing motivating goals to tracking your progress and celebrating your achievements, we'll provide practical guidance to help you stay focused, motivated, and accountable along the way.

Establishing Realistic and Motivating Reading Goals.

Setting reading goals is like charting a course for your literary adventure—it gives you direction and purpose as you navigate the vast sea of books. Here's how to establish goals that are both achievable and inspiring:

Identify Your Interests and Aspirations: Start by reflecting on your interests, passions, and aspirations as a reader. What genres do you enjoy? Are there any authors or topics you're curious about exploring? By understanding what drives your reading journey, you can tailor your goals to align with your personal preferences and aspirations.

Set Specific and Measurable Goals: Be clear and specific about what you want to achieve with your reading. Whether it's reading a certain number of books, exploring a new genre, or delving into a specific topic, set goals that are concrete and measurable so you can track your progress effectively.

Establish Realistic Timelines: Consider your schedule, commitments, and reading habits when setting timelines for your goals. Be realistic about how much time you can dedicate to reading each day or week, and adjust your goals accordingly to ensure they are achievable within your available time frame.

Breaking Down Larger Reading Goals into Manageable Milestones.

Large reading goals can seem daunting at first glance, but breaking them down into smaller milestones can make them more manageable and achievable. Here's how to divide your goals into bite-sized steps:

Break it Down into Smaller Tasks: Divide your larger reading goals into smaller, more manageable tasks or milestones. For example, if your goal is to read 50 books in a year, break it down into reading approximately one book per week or setting monthly reading targets.

Set Deadlines for Milestones: Assign deadlines or target dates for each milestone to create a sense of urgency and accountability. Having specific deadlines will help you stay on track and ensure steady progress towards your larger goal.

Celebrate Achievements Along the Way: Celebrate each milestone you reach along your reading journey to acknowledge your progress and stay motivated. Whether it's finishing a book, reaching a monthly reading target, or exploring a new genre, take time to celebrate your achievements and pat yourself on the back for your hard work and dedication.

Tracking Progress and Celebrating Achievements

Tracking your reading progress is essential for staying motivated and accountable. Here's how to monitor your progress and celebrate your achievements:

Use a Reading Journal or Tracker: Keep a reading journal or use a reading tracker app to record the books you've read, track your reading progress, and jot down any thoughts or reflections about your reading experience.

Review Your Goals Regularly: Take time to review your reading goals regularly to assess your progress and make any necessary adjustments. Reflect on what's working well and what challenges you're facing, and adjust your goals or strategies accordingly to stay on track.

Celebrate Your Achievements: When you reach a milestone or achieve a reading goal, take time to celebrate your accomplishments. Treat yourself to a small reward, share your achievement with friends or family, or simply take a moment to bask in the satisfaction of reaching your goal.

setting and achieving reading goals is a journey of self-discovery and personal growth. By establishing realistic and motivating goals, breaking them down into manageable milestones, tracking your progress, and celebrating your achievements along the way, you can embark on a fulfilling reading journey that enriches your mind, expands your horizons, and brings you endless joy and satisfaction.

CHAPTER 10:

Training Yourself to Enjoy the Reading Habit.

In this chapter, we'll explore strategies to help you cultivate a love for reading and turn it into a fun and enjoyable habit. Whether you're a reluctant reader looking to reignite your passion for books or a newcomer eager to develop a lifelong reading habit, these tips will guide you on your journey to becoming a joyful reader.

How to Make Reading a Fun Habit

Start Small and Build Momentum: Begin by setting achievable reading goals that are easy to accomplish. Instead of aiming to read for hours at a time, start with shorter reading sessions, such as 10 or 15 minutes a day. By starting small, you'll build momentum and gradually increase your reading stamina over time.

Choose Books That Spark Your Interest: Select books that captivate your curiosity and align with your interests and passions. Whether it's a thrilling mystery, a heartwarming romance, or a fascinating non-fiction topic, choose books that excite you and make you eager to dive into the story.

Create a Cozy Reading Environment: Designate a comfortable and inviting space where you can curl up with a good book and escape into the world of imagination. Surround yourself with soft blankets, plush pillows, and soothing lighting to create a cozy atmosphere that enhances your reading experience.

Experiment with Different Formats: Explore various reading formats, such as print books, e-books, and audiobooks, to discover what works best for you. Some people enjoy the tactile experience of holding a physical book, while others prefer the convenience of digital formats or the immersive experience of audiobooks. Experimenting with different formats can make reading more enjoyable and accessible.

Set Aside Dedicated Reading Time: Schedule regular reading sessions into your daily routine and treat them as sacred moments of relaxation and enjoyment. Whether it's in the morning before work, during your lunch break, or before bed, carve out dedicated time for reading and make it a priority in your schedule.

Find a Reading Buddy: Share your reading journey with a friend, family member, or book club member who shares your love of literature. Reading together, discussing books, and exchanging recommendations can make reading more enjoyable and foster a sense of camaraderie and connection.

Mix Up Your Reading Routine: Keep your reading experience fresh and exciting by mixing up your reading routine. Try reading in different locations, such as a park, coffee shop, or library, to change up the scenery and stimulate your senses. You can also experiment with different genres, authors, and formats to keep your reading experience varied and engaging.

Set Reading Challenges and Rewards: Challenge yourself to reach reading milestones or complete reading challenges, such as reading a certain number of books in a month or exploring a new genre. Reward yourself with small treats or incentives for reaching your goals, such as treating yourself to a favorite snack or indulging in a cozy night of reading by the fireplace.

Embrace the Joy of Reading: Above all, remember to have fun and enjoy the experience of getting lost in a good book. Reading should be a pleasurable escape, a chance to explore new worlds, learn new things, and connect with characters and stories that captivate your imagination.

training yourself to enjoy the reading habit is all about making reading a fun and rewarding part of your daily life. By starting small, choosing books that spark your interest, creating a cozy reading environment, experimenting with different formats, setting aside dedicated reading time, finding a reading buddy, mixing up your reading routine, and setting reading challenges and rewards, you can cultivate a love for reading that brings joy, fulfillment, and endless adventure.

PART THREE:

Understanding the Benefits of Reading.

Reading is not merely a pastime; it is a gateway to personal growth and enrichment. In this chapter, we delve into the myriad advantages that reading offers to individuals of all ages and backgrounds. reading expands our horizons by exposing us to new ideas, cultures, and perspectives. Whether through fiction, non-fiction, or poetry, books provide us with a window into worlds beyond our own, fostering empathy and understanding in the process.

Enhancing Vocabulary and Cognitive Skills.

At the heart of every great reader lies a vast treasury of words, waiting to be unleashed upon the world. Through the act of reading, we expand our lexicon, imbuing our speech and writing with nuance, eloquence, and precision. Research conducted by the National Endowment for the Arts has shown a direct correlation between reading proficiency and academic success, highlighting the pivotal role that vocabulary acquisition plays in cognitive development.

Fostering Empathy and Emotional Intelligence.

Step into the shoes of another, and behold the transformative power of empathy. Through the vicarious experiences of characters in literature, we gain insight into the rich tapestry of human emotions—joy, sorrow, love, and despair. Studies conducted by psychologists such as Raymond Mar and Keith Oatley have demonstrated that reading fiction enhances our capacity for empathy, enabling us to navigate the complexities of human relationships with grace and understanding.

Alleviating Stress and Promoting Mental Well-Being.

In the tranquil embrace of a captivating story lies respite from the tumult of daily life. The rhythmic cadence of words soothes the restless mind, transporting us to realms of imagination and wonder. Scientific research conducted by the University of Sussex has shown that just six minutes of reading can reduce stress levels by up to 68%, making it a potent antidote to the anxieties that plague our modern existence.

Stimulating the Mind: Exercise for the Brain.

Just as physical exercise is essential for maintaining physical health, mental exercise is crucial for preserving cognitive function and warding off age-related cognitive decline. And what better workout for the brain than the intricate dance of comprehension and imagination elicited by the act of reading? Studies in neuroscience have revealed that reading stimulates multiple regions of the brain involved in language processing, visual imagery, and executive function, thereby sharpening cognitive faculties and enhancing overall brain health.

Furthermore, the cognitive demands inherent in navigating complex narratives and deciphering unfamiliar vocabulary contribute to the development of cognitive flexibility, problem-solving skills, and creative thinking abilities. In essence, reading is not merely a leisurely pastime but a cognitive workout of the highest order—one that challenges the mind, enriches the soul, and nourishes the intellect.

In conclusion, the benefits of reading are as diverse and profound as the stories themselves. From enriching vocabulary and enhancing empathy to reducing stress and stimulating the mind, the transformative power of books knows no bounds.

CHAPTER 11:

Overcoming Common Barriers to Reading.

In the midst of our busy lives, finding time to read can feel like trying to catch a breeze in a whirlwind. We're pulled in countless directions, leaving little room for the simple pleasure of sitting down with a book. But fear not! In this chapter, we'll explore the common obstacles that stand in the way of our reading habits and unveil practical strategies to overcome them.

Obstacles That Hinder Reading Habits:

Lack of Time: Time is a precious resource, and it often feels like there's never enough of it. Between work, school, family, and other commitments, finding a spare moment to read can seem impossible.

Distractions: In today's digital age, distractions are everywhere. Whether it's notifications on our phones, social media scrolling, or the allure of television, staying focused on reading can be a challenge.

Difficulty Focusing: Even when we do carve out time to read, focusing on the words on the page can be tough. Our minds wander, and before we know it, we've read the same paragraph five times without absorbing a word.

Practical Strategies for Overcoming These Barriers:

Setting Aside Dedicated Reading Time: Just as we schedule appointments and meetings, we can set aside specific blocks of time for reading. Whether it's ten minutes before bed or during your lunch break, making reading a priority helps ensure it doesn't get lost in the shuffle of daily life.

Minimizing Distractions: Identify the biggest distractions in your environment and take steps to minimize them. This might mean turning off notifications on your phone, finding a quiet space to read, or using noise-canceling headphones to block out background noise.

Choosing Engaging Books: Not all books are created equal when it comes to holding our attention. Choose books that align with your interests and passions, and don't be afraid to abandon a book that isn't capturing your attention. Reading should be enjoyable, not a chore.

By implementing these simple strategies, you can overcome the common barriers that hinder your reading habits and unlock the joy of getting lost in a good book. Remember, reading is not just a pastime—it's a gateway to new worlds, new ideas, and new possibilities. So make time for it, eliminate distractions, and choose books that speak to your soul. Your inner bookworm will thank you!

CHAPTER 12:

Choosing the Right Books.

Selecting the perfect book is like embarking on a journey—one filled with excitement, discovery, and endless possibilities. In this chapter, we'll delve into the art of choosing books that resonate with you, cater to your interests, and align with your reading goals. Whether you're a seasoned bibliophile or just dipping your toes into the vast ocean of literature, these simple yet effective strategies will guide you on your quest for the perfect read.

Guide to Selecting Books that Align with You:

Know Thyself: The first step in choosing the right book is to understand your own interests, preferences, and reading goals. Are you drawn to mystery and suspense, or do you prefer heartwarming romance? Do you crave thought-provoking non-fiction or escapist fantasy? Take some time to reflect on what genres, themes, and styles appeal to you the most.

Explore Your Passions: Consider books that align with your passions and hobbies. If you're a history buff, delve into historical fiction or non-fiction. If you love cooking, explore culinary memoirs or recipe collections. By connecting your reading choices to your interests, you'll find deeper enjoyment and fulfillment in your literary pursuits.

Seek Recommendations: Don't be afraid to ask for recommendations from friends, family, or fellow book lovers. They can offer valuable insights and introduce you to books you might not have discovered on your own. Book recommendation websites, such as Goodreads or BookBub, are also excellent resources for discovering new reads tailored to your tastes.

Explore Diverse Genres, Authors, and Formats:

Genre Exploration: Step outside your comfort zone and explore diverse genres to expand your reading horizons. From science fiction and fantasy to mystery, romance, and literary fiction, there's a wealth of genres waiting to be explored. Don't limit yourself to familiar territory—venture into uncharted literary terrain and discover hidden gems along the way.

Author Spotlight: Discover new authors whose writing style and storytelling resonate with you. Keep an eye out for award-winning authors or explore debut novels for fresh voices and perspectives. Following your favorite authors on social media or subscribing to author newsletters can also provide insights into their latest releases and upcoming projects.

Format Flexibility: Consider experimenting with different book formats to enhance your reading experience. Whether you prefer traditional print books, e-books, audiobooks, or graphic novels, each format offers a unique way to engage with the story. Embrace the versatility of modern technology and explore which format best suits your lifestyle and preferences.

Discovering New Books:

Join Book Clubs: Book clubs are a fantastic way to connect with other readers, discover new books, and engage in lively discussions. Look for local book clubs in your community or join online book clubs focused on specific genres or themes. Sharing your reading experiences with others can enrich your literary journey and foster a sense of community.

Online Communities: Engage with online communities and forums dedicated to book lovers. Platforms like Reddit's r/books or Bookstagram on Instagram offer opportunities to connect with fellow readers, share book recommendations, and participate in reading challenges and discussions. These virtual communities provide a welcoming space for bibliophiles to connect and share their love of reading.

Recommendation Websites: Explore book recommendation websites and platforms tailored to your reading preferences. Websites like Goodreads, BookBub, and LibraryThing offer personalized book recommendations based on your past reading history and preferences. Discover new releases, bestsellers, and hidden gems recommended by fellow readers and literary experts.

By following these simple yet effective strategies, you'll be well-equipped to choose books that resonate with you, cater to your interests, and enrich your reading experience. Remember, the journey of choosing the right book is just as rewarding as the destination.

CHAPTER 13:

Developing a Reading Routine.

Consistency is the cornerstone of building any habit, and reading is no exception. In this chapter, we'll explore why establishing a regular reading routine is crucial for cultivating a lifelong love of books. We'll also delve into practical advice and actionable tips to help you create a reading routine that fits seamlessly into your daily life.

Understanding the Importance of Consistency:

Building Momentum: Just like a rolling stone gathers no moss, consistent reading builds momentum over time. By making reading a regular part of your routine, you gradually develop a habit that becomes second nature—a habit that enriches your life and expands your horizons.

Deepening Engagement: Consistent reading allows you to immerse yourself fully in the world of books, fostering a deeper connection with the stories, characters, and ideas within. As you engage with books on a regular basis, you'll find yourself more invested in the reading experience, leading to greater enjoyment and satisfaction.

Cultivating Discipline: Consistency breeds discipline, and discipline is the bedrock of personal growth and achievement. By committing to a regular reading routine, you exercise self-discipline and strengthen your ability to stay focused and motivated—a skill that transcends the realm of reading and permeates every aspect of your life.

Practical Advice for Establishing a Reading Routine:

Set Clear Goals: Start by defining your reading goals—whether it's to read a certain number of books per month, explore a specific genre, or tackle a reading challenge. Having clear goals provides direction and motivation, guiding your reading choices and keeping you on track.

Create a Reading Schedule: Allocate dedicated time for reading in your daily or weekly schedule. Whether it's early in the morning, during your lunch break, or before bedtime, find a time that works best for you and stick to it. Treat your reading time as non-negotiable—an essential appointment with yourself and your books.

Incorporate Reading into Daily Rituals: Integrate reading into your daily rituals and routines to make it a natural and enjoyable part of your day. Whether it's sipping your morning coffee with a book in hand, listening to audiobooks during your commute, or winding down with a chapter before bed, find moments throughout the day to indulge in the pleasure of reading.

Start Small and Build Consistency: If you're just starting out, don't overwhelm yourself with lofty reading goals. Begin with small, manageable targets and gradually increase them as your reading routine becomes more ingrained. Even just a few minutes of reading each day can make a significant difference over time.

Stay Flexible and Adapt: Life is unpredictable, and there will be days when your reading routine gets derailed. Be flexible and adaptable—forgive yourself for missed reading sessions and pick up where you left off. The key is not perfection but persistence—consistently showing up and making reading a priority, no matter what.

By implementing these practical tips and strategies, you'll be well on your way to developing a reading routine that enhances your life, nourishes your mind, and brings you endless joy and fulfillment. Remember, consistency is the secret ingredient that transforms reading from a sporadic activity into a lifelong passion.

CHAPTER 14:

Active Reading Strategies.

Reading isn't just about passively consuming words on a page—it's about actively engaging with the material, delving deep into the text, and forging a meaningful connection with the ideas and insights it contains. In this chapter, we'll explore techniques for active reading that will enhance your comprehension, retention, and overall enjoyment of books. From annotating and summarizing to reflecting and questioning, these strategies will empower you to become an active participant in the reading process.

Introducing Active Reading Techniques:

Annotating: Annotation is the act of marking up a text with notes, highlights, and comments to aid comprehension and engagement. As you read, jot down key points, underline important passages, and write down your thoughts and questions in the margins. Annotation not only helps you stay focused and actively involved in the text but also serves as a valuable reference for future review and reflection.

Summarizing: Summarization involves distilling the main ideas and key points of a text into concise summaries. After reading a section or chapter, take a moment to summarize the main ideas in your own words. This process helps reinforce your understanding of the material and encourages deeper engagement with the text.

Reflecting: Reflection is the process of pausing to consider the significance of what you've read and how it relates to your own experiences, beliefs, and values. After finishing a chapter or book, take some time to reflect on the insights gained, the lessons learned, and the questions raised. Ask yourself how the material resonates with you personally and what implications it may have for your life or worldview.

Guidance for Improving Comprehension and Retention:

Stay Focused: Maintain focus and concentration while reading by minimizing distractions and creating a conducive environment for learning. Find a quiet space free from interruptions, turn off electronic devices, and set aside dedicated time for reading without distractions.

Active Engagement: Actively engage with the text by asking questions, making predictions, and forming connections between ideas. Challenge yourself to think critically about the material and consider alternative viewpoints or interpretations.

Review and Recap: Periodically review and recap what you've read to reinforce your understanding and retention of the material. Create summary notes, flashcards, or concept maps to organize key concepts and information, and use them as study aids for future reference.

Practice Active Recall: Test your comprehension and retention by actively recalling and summarizing key points from memory. After reading a section or chapter, try to summarize the main ideas without referring back to the text. This exercise strengthens your memory and reinforces your understanding of the material.

Discuss and Share: Engage in discussions with others about the books you're reading, whether it's with friends, family, or fellow book club members. Sharing your insights and perspectives with others not only deepens your understanding of the material but also provides valuable opportunities for reflection and learning.

By incorporating these active reading strategies into your reading routine, you'll not only enhance your comprehension and retention of the material but also develop a deeper appreciation for the richness and complexity of the books you encounter. Remember, reading is not a passive activity—it's a dynamic and interactive process that invites you to explore, question, and engage with the world of ideas.

CHAPTER 15:

Balancing Reading with Technology.

In today's fast-paced world, technology has become an integral part of our lives, transforming the way we consume information and engage with the written word. In this chapter, we'll explore the evolving relationship between technology and reading habits, examining both its benefits and drawbacks. We'll also discuss practical strategies for finding a healthy balance between screen time and traditional reading, ensuring that technology enhances rather than detracts from our literary pursuits.

The Role of Technology in Modern Reading Habits:

Accessibility and Convenience: One of the most significant benefits of technology is its ability to make reading more accessible and convenient. With e-readers, tablets, and smartphones, we can carry entire libraries in our pockets, access a vast array of books instantly, and read anytime, anywhere.

Enhanced Interactivity: Technology has revolutionized the reading experience, introducing features like interactive e-books, audiobooks, and multimedia content. These interactive elements can enhance comprehension, engagement, and accessibility, particularly for readers with diverse learning styles or accessibility needs.

Community and Connection: The digital age has facilitated the creation of online reading communities, where readers can connect, share recommendations, and engage in discussions about books. Social media platforms, book blogs, and online forums provide opportunities for readers to connect with like-minded individuals and discover new books and authors.

Potential Benefits and Drawbacks of Technology:

◇ **Benefits:**
◇ Accessibility to a vast array of books.
◇ Enhanced interactivity and multimedia features.
◇ Connection with online reading communities.
◇ **Drawbacks:**
◇ Digital distractions and information overload.
◇ Eye strain and fatigue from prolonged screen time.
◇ Potential loss of deep, immersive reading experiences.

Strategies for Finding a Healthy Balance:

Set Boundaries: Establish boundaries around your technology use, such as designated screen-free times or digital detox days. Create a balance between screen time for work or leisure and dedicated time for traditional reading.

Practice Mindful Reading: When engaging with digital devices, practice mindfulness and intentionality. Avoid multitasking and immerse yourself fully in the reading experience, focusing on the words on the screen and the story unfolding before you.

Prioritize Traditional Books: Make a conscious effort to prioritize reading traditional print books or e-ink devices over screens with backlighting, as they are less likely to cause eye strain and disrupt sleep patterns.

Limit Screen Exposure Before Bed: Reduce exposure to screens before bedtime to promote better sleep quality and avoid the negative effects of blue light on melatonin production. Opt for a traditional book or an e-ink device with adjustable brightness settings for bedtime reading.

Engage in Digital Detoxes: Periodically disconnect from digital devices and engage in digital detoxes to recharge your mind and reconnect with the physical world. Use this time to immerse yourself in traditional reading, outdoor activities, or other offline hobbies.

while technology offers numerous benefits for modern readers, it's essential to strike a balance between screen time and traditional reading to ensure a fulfilling and enriching reading experience. By implementing mindful reading practices and setting boundaries around technology use, we can harness the benefits of technology while preserving the joy and depth of traditional reading.

Conclusion:

Embarking on Your Reading Adventure.

As we draw the final pages of our book, let's reflect on the enriching journey we've embarked on together and summarize the valuable lessons we've learned along the way. Here's a simple breakdown of our key takeaways:

1. Discover Your Reading Preferences: We've explored the vast landscape of literature, encouraging you to explore different genres, authors, and styles to find what truly captivates your interest. Whether it's diving into thrilling mysteries, heartwarming romances, or thought-provoking non-fiction, discovering your reading niche adds an extra layer of enjoyment to your reading experience.

2. Create Your Perfect Reading Space: Designing a cozy and inviting reading environment sets the stage for a delightful reading experience. We've discussed how elements like lighting, seating arrangements, and ambiance can transform any corner of your home into a sanctuary where you can escape into the pages of a good book.

3. Set Attainable Reading Goals: By setting realistic reading goals and breaking them down into manageable milestones, you can track your progress and celebrate your achievements along the way. Whether it's aiming to read a certain number of books in a year or exploring new genres, setting goals keeps you motivated and focused on your reading journey.

4. Make Reading an Enjoyable Habit: Reading should be a source of pleasure and relaxation, not a chore. We've shared tips on how to make reading fun, from joining book clubs and trying different formats to rewarding yourself for reaching reading milestones. Embracing the joy of reading adds excitement and fulfillment to your daily life.

5. Embrace the Adventure: Above all, we encourage you to approach your reading journey with confidence and enthusiasm. Let your curiosity guide you as you explore new worlds, learn new things, and connect with characters and stories that touch your heart. Remember that each book is a gateway to endless possibilities and discoveries.

As we bid farewell, we express our deepest gratitude for joining us on this quest to cultivate enjoyable reading habits. Your companionship on this literary adventure has been a joy and an honor. We hope that the insights shared within these pages will inspire you to continue your reading journey with passion, curiosity, and an open heart.

So, dear reader, as you close this book and embark on your next reading adventure, may you journey with confidence, enthusiasm, and a sense of wonder. Happy reading, and may your love for books continue to grow and flourish with each turn of the page.

Milton Keynes UK
Ingram Content Group UK Ltd.
UKHW020316100424
440866UK00014B/341

9 798224 970827